AMERICAN MUSEUM
ᵒ̄ NATURAL HISTORY
EASY READERS

Baby Whale's
Long Swim

Connie and Peter Roop

STERLING CHILDREN'S BOOKS
New York

It is winter in Mexico.

The water is warm and clear.

NOTE TO PARENTS

Learning to read is an important skill for all children. It is a big milestone that you can help your child reach. The American Museum of Natural History Easy Reader program is designed to support you and your child through this process. Developed by reading specialists, each book in the series includes carefully selected words and sentence structures to help children advance from beginner to intermediate to proficient readers.

Here are some tips to keep in mind as you read these books with your child:

First, preview the book together. Read the title. Then look at the cover. Ask your child, "What is happening on the cover? What do you think this book is about?"

Next, skim through the pages of the book and look at the illustrations. This will help your child use the illustrations to understand the story.

Then encourage your child to read. If he or she stumbles over words, try some of these strategies:

- use the pictures as clues
- point out words that are repeated
- sound out difficult words
- break up bigger words into smaller chunks
- use the context to lend meaning

Finally, find out if your child understands what he or she is reading. After you have finished reading, ask, "What happened in this book?"

Above all, understand that each child learns to read at a different rate. Make sure to praise your young reader and provide encouragement along the way!

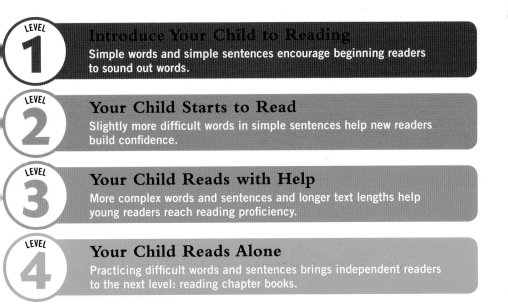

LEVEL 1

Introduce Your Child to Reading
Simple words and simple sentences encourage beginning readers to sound out words.

LEVEL 2

Your Child Starts to Read
Slightly more difficult words in simple sentences help new readers build confidence.

LEVEL 3

Your Child Reads with Help
More complex words and sentences and longer text lengths help young readers reach reading proficiency.

LEVEL 4

Your Child Reads Alone
Practicing difficult words and sentences brings independent readers to the next level: reading chapter books.

*For Sterling and Meaghan as they "migrate" around the world.
And for Sadie and Simon as they grow and learn!
—C.R. and P.R.*

Photo credits

Cover/title page: © Richard Herrmann/SeaPics.com
Pages 4–5: © Pacific Stock/SuperStock; 6–7: © AnimalsAnimals/SuperStock; 8–9: © François Gohier/ardea.com;
10: © Mark Carwadine/naturepl.com; 11: © AridOcean/shutterstock; 12–13: © Marilyn & Maris Kazmers/SeaPics.com;
14–15: © Doc White/SeaPics.com; 16–17: © François Gohier/ardea.com; 18–19: © Michael Nolan/age footstock;
20–21: © Michael Nolan/age footstock; 22: © age fotostock/SuperStock; 23: © Peggy Stap/SeaPics.com;
24–25: © Sue Flood/npl/Minden Pictures; 26–27: © Jocrebbin/Dreamstime.com;
28: © Michio Hoshino/Minden Pictures/National Geographic Stock; 29: © Jocrebbin/Dreamstime.com;
30: © AridOcean/shutterstock; 31: © Mark Carwadine/naturepl.com;
32: © Nick Voss

STERLING CHILDREN'S BOOKS
New York

An Imprint of Sterling Publishing
387 Park Avenue South
New York, NY 10016

STERLING CHILDREN'S BOOKS and the distinctive Sterling Children's Books logo
are trademarks of Sterling Publishing Co., Inc.

© 2012 by Sterling Publishing Co., Inc., and
The American Museum of Natural History

ISBN 978-1-4027-9111-6 (hardcover) *4973 7314*
ISBN 978-1-4027-7786-8 (paperback)

10/12

Distributed in Canada by Sterling Publishing
c/o Canadian Manda Group, 165 Dufferin Street
Toronto, Ontario, Canada M6K 3H6
Distributed in the United Kingdom by GMC Distribution Services
Castle Place, 166 High Street, Lewes, East Sussex, England BN7 1XU
Distributed in Australia by Capricorn Link (Australia) Pty. Ltd.
P.O. Box 704, Windsor, NSW 2756, Australia

For information about custom editions, special sales, and premium and corporate purchases,
please contact Sterling Special Sales at 800-805-5489 or specialsales@sterlingpublishing.com.

Printed in China
Lot #:
2 4 6 8 10 9 7 5 3 1
01/12

www.sterlingpublishing.com/kids

FREE ACTIVITIES & PUZZLES ONLINE AT
http://www.sterlingpublishing.com/kids/sterlingeventkits

A baby gray whale swims with
his mother.

He drinks her milk so he can grow.

A baby whale is called a calf.

The mother pushes her calf up, up, up!

She pushes him to the top of the water.

The calf takes a breath of air.

He breathes through a blowhole

on the top of his head.

The blowhole is like your nostrils.

The calf can close the blowhole

to keep water out.

It is spring now.

The calf and his mother swim north.

There is food for them in Alaska.

This map shows a gray whale's trip from Mexico to Alaska.

Gray whales swim to Alaska
and back every year.
It takes them four months
just to get there.

Some swim in a group, called a pod.

Some swim alone.

The mother and her calf swim

together with the pod.

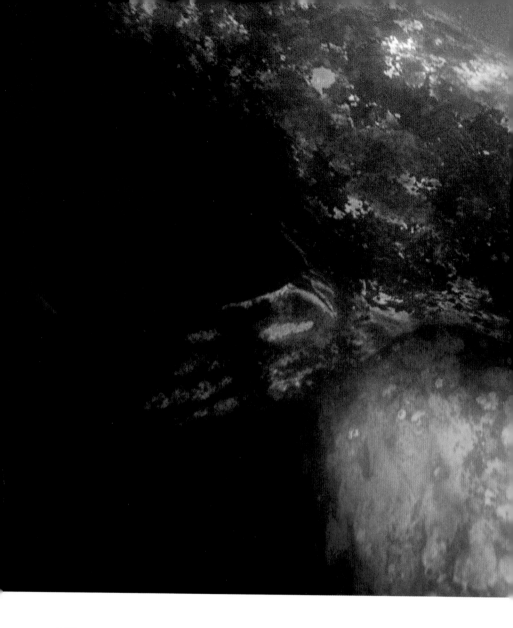

The baby gray whale is tired.

He has been swimming for a long time.

He rests against his mother.

The calf and his mother lift their
heads out of the water and look
all around.

All clear!

There is no danger.

The calf jumps out of the water.

This is called breaching.

The whales swim for many days.

They roll on their sides.

They wave their fins.

Oh, no!

A hungry black and white orca

swims close.

An orca is another kind of whale.

The orca wants to hurt them.

The gray whale mother fights with

the orca!

The gray whale wins the fight.

She protects her calf.

The black and white orca swims away.

The mother and calf keep swimming to Alaska.

They dive down.

The mother's tail hits the water.

SPLASH!

The mother and calf reach Alaska.

It is an icy summer here.

The whales catch tiny plants and
animals in their mouths.

Their mouths have edges like a comb.

Food gets trapped there.

The summer is over.

The gray whale calf and his mother

will swim back to Mexico.

It is time for another long trip!

MEET THE EXPERT!

My name is **Dr. Nancy Simmons**, and I am a curator at the American Museum of Natural History. I study the anatomy and evolution of mammals. I do research mainly on bats, but I have always enjoyed learning about whales, too. I began scuba diving in college and have been lucky enough to see whales in their native habitat. As a child, I enjoyed collecting natural objects, including fossils, bird nests, butterflies, leaves, seashells, and animal bones. This is what led me to become a mammal specialist as an adult.

One of the things that has always fascinated me is the bone structure of different animals. Bones tell much of the story of how an animal lives. Whale skeletons, for example, have front legs and hands that are shaped like paddles and help whales move in the water. They have a specialized tail that helps them swim. Whale skulls have nostrils on top—that's the blowhole.

I am fortunate to have a job where I get to work with bones and study living animals in the field. As an expert on bats, I do field research in the rain forests of South America and Central America. In this work I go out at night and catch as many as 100 bats! It's exciting to be among them and see their behavior up close. Working for the Museum, I have stayed up all night many times, worked in the rain, and been bitten by vampire bats—but I still think I have the best job in the world!